The New Protectionists: The Privatisation of US Trade Policy

Marcus Noland
Senior Fellow, Institute for International Economics

Published by the IEA Trade and Development Unit, 1999

First published in October 1999 by
The Trade and Development Unit
The Institute of Economic Affairs
2 Lord North Street
Westminster
London SW1P 3LB

Copyright by the Institute for International Economics.
All rights reserved

IEA Studies in Trade and Development No. 3
ISBN 0-255 364679

Printed in Great Britain by
Hartington Fine Arts Limited, Lancing, West Sussex
Set in Times New Roman and Univers

Contents

	Foreword	*Gerald Frost*	5
	The Author		8
1.	Introduction		9
2.	**The Changing Bias of Trade Protection**		12
3.	**New Issues and Players**		15
	The NAFTA Debate		16
	Labour and Human Rights Clauses		18
	Trade Policy and Environmental Protection		19
	Economic Sanctions and Foreign Policy Goals		21
	The Case of the MAI		22
4.	**Constraints on Unilateralism**		24
	Bananas and WTO Rules		25
5.	**Fast-track Authority and the Role of the Judiciary**		27
6.	**Conclusion**		31

Foreword

America's conversion to free trade lay at the foundation of the post-Second Word War economic growth in which all western countries shared. Through numerous negotiating rounds the General Agreement on Tariffs and Trade (GATT) was able to bring down average tariff rates from around 40 per cent to around 4 per cent today. Reduced tariffs permitted the expansion of world trade from $100 billion in 1960 to $6.5 trillion in 1998.

The present pattern of growing economic interdependence ('globalisation') is a reflection of this more open trading environment as well as a reason for believing that further increases in international trade flows are likely. In turn, these may be expected to facilitate further advances in growth and living standards. Such advances, however, plainly depend upon a continued commitment to free trade by the world's greatest economic player. This requires that American policymakers both respond robustly to a range of new challenges to a liberal trading order, and display a greater readiness to explain the benefits of free trade to the US public. But there are reasons for thinking that this cannot be taken for granted. Indeed, in the view of Dr Marcus Noland, the author of Studies in Trade and Development Number 3, the advocates of free trade, both those within American government and those outside it, have been comprehensively outplayed by special interest groups. These groups have effectively 'privatised' trade policy, largely for reasons unconnected with trade, and without regard to the economic consequences of their actions. Government has reacted to this situation on an *ad hoc* basis; the result is a policy which displays little coherence and consequently enjoys little public support.

Historically, trade policy had been the responsibility of Congress. But for half a century, beginning in 1934, as Dr Noland points out, Congress permitted the President to take the lead in formulating policy, latterly through the Office of the US

Trade Representative. This arrangement avoided the dangers arising from the tendency of congressmen to engage in protectionist log-rolling exercises, a temptation to which they had succumbed during the inter-war years and with deeply unfortunate consequences.

From the mid-1980s, however, the present system began to break down as a result of a range of developments which greatly complicated policy formulation, including the anxieties and pressures generated by the increase in the US trade deficit to historically unprecedented levels. As Dr Noland explains, earlier pressures of this kind had led to unilateral actions to pry open foreign markets against those countries with which the US ran the greatest deficits. But the dispute settlements procedures of the World Trade Organisation (WTO), which are considerably stronger than those of the GATT, greatly discourage the use of traditional remedies; in their absence the executive is faced by demands to protect US industry from foreign competition in other ways.

A second complicating factor is the emergence of new issues, especially in the areas of environmental and human rights, and the consequent involvement of new players, especially non-governmental organisations. In several instances these players have found common cause with traditional and business lobbies, and have used judicial as well as political routes to achieve particular policy outcomes. The emergence of environmental issues has also led to the establishment of interagency policy-making bodies within government with a voice on trade issues; this, Dr Noland argues, considerably enhanced the prospect of 'cross-issue' log-rolling.

Foremost among those new purposes to which trade policy is put is its growing use as an instrument of foreign policy – with the remarkable result that the US currently imposes sanctions against 26 countries, accounting for more than half the world's population. This enables the federal and even sub-federal government to strike moral postures in response to the behaviour of régimes which they find morally reprehensible. But, as Dr Nolan argues, although a sanctions-happy foreign policy may have the effect of imposing terrible costs on populations that may have little or no influence on the régimes against which the measures are directed, their impact on the US is considerable: it is to reduce exports by $20 billion and to destroy as many as 200,000 jobs annually. There is also little evidence that trade sanctions achieve their goals, as the political survival of Fidel Castro and Saddam Hussein amply demonstrates.

In this new and infinitely more complex policy-making environment greater coherence might be achieved by either of two means: by recognising the salience of the new issues through a revised political agenda, or by insulating the market process from the new demands. In Dr Noland's view, neither course is likely to be followed; a more likely outcome is the continued hijacking of trade policy by narrow special interest groups and increasing incoherence in the aims and overall direction of policy. In the conditions that prevail, the best that can be hoped for is a series of international agreements which pre-commit the US government to relatively enlightened policies. But, as Dr Noland ruefully acknowledges, even this will require greater intellectual courage on the part of those who support a liberal international trading regime than they have recently displayed.

The IEA does not seek to express a common view through its publications. The views expressed in its publications are those of the authors, not of the Institute, its Trustees, Advisers or Directors. We are grateful to Dr Noland for so ably bringing to light new sources of trade protectionism, and for explaining the much greater complexities with which those responsible for US trade policy must now grapple.

July 1999   GERALD FROST
Director, IEA Trade and Development Unit

The Author

Marcus Noland was educated at Swarthmore College (BA) and the Johns Hopkins University (PhD). He is currently a Senior Fellow at the Institute for International Economics. He was a Senior Economist at the Council of Economic Advisers in the Executive Office of the President of the United States, and has held research or teaching positions at the Johns Hopkins University, the University of Southern California, Tokyo University, Saitama University, the University of Ghana, and the Korea Development Institute. He has been the recipient of fellowships sponsored by the Japan Society for the Promotion of Science, the Council on Foreign Relations, and the Council for the International Exchange of Scholars.

Noland is the co-author (with Bela Balassa) of *Japan in the World Economy*, the author of *Pacific Basin Developing Countries: Prospects for the Future*, co-editor (with C. Fred Bergsten) *of Pacific Dynamism and the International Economic System*, co-author (with Bergsten) of *Reconcilable Differences? Resolving United States – Japan Economic Conflict*, editor of *Economic Integration of the Korean Peninsula*, and co-author (with LiGang Liu, Sherman Robinson, and Zhi Wang) of *Global Economic Effects of the Asian Currency Devaluations*, all published by the Institute for International Economics. In addition to these books he has written many scholarly articles on international economics, US trade policy, and the economies of the Asia-Pacific region. He also has served as an occasional consultant to organisations as varied as the World Bank, the New York Stock Exchange, and the International Food Policy Research Institute, and has testified before the US Congress on numerous occasions.

1. Introduction

When time came for Pat Buchanan to launch his third campaign for the presidency of the US, the protectionist Buchanan visited Weirton, West Virginia, the archetypal steel town. Weirton, buffeted by a surge in imported steel, was a natural backdrop for Buchanan's protectionist fulminations. But 'Pitchfork Pat' had a predecessor: six years earlier, then presidential candidate Bill Clinton came to town, promising, in the pursuit of fair trade, to uphold the anti-dumping laws of the US. That both the hapless Buchanan and the ultimately triumphant Clinton felt compelled to invoke the symbolism of a decaying steel town in articulating their respective trade policy positions speaks volumes about the lack of clarity in the public discussion of trade in the US today. In the political sphere, American free traders lack the courage of their convictions, and this has permitted the terms of the public discussion to be defined by a growing plethora of narrow special interest groups which seek to use trade policy to further their own particular ends.

The US is a large, diverse, multiethnic, immigrant-based democracy. Its political institutions and culture reflect the emphasis on access and procedural transparency to promote a sense of inclusion and fairness necessary for social and political stability in such a society. The Constitution of the US vests in the Congress the power to 'regulate Commerce with foreign Nations,' prohibits the levying of export taxes, and specifies that 'all bills for raising revenue' will originate in the House of Representatives, the lower or more immediately populist or politicised body of its bicameral legislature. As a consequence, the House's fiscal committee, the Committee on Ways and Means, has historically taken the lead in framing US trade policy.

For much of the nation's history, this amounted to setting import tariffs on manufactures to encourage import-substituting industrialisation in a late developer. The process proved amenable to log-rolling, however, culminating in the high levels of protection embodied in the Fordney–McCumber Act of 1922 and infamous Smoot–Hawley Act of 1930, the last comprehensive tariff ever passed by the US Congress in which individual legislators traded votes on specific tariff lines.

The Smoot–Hawley fiasco and its role in the Great Depression led to a political reaction in the US. In 1934, the Congress passed the Reciprocal Trade Agreements Act which ushered in a five-decade era mainly characterised by Congressional quiescence on trade policy. The locus of policy-making shifted away from the Congress to the presidential administrative apparatus, initially to the Department of State, and later to the Office of the Special Trade Representative, renamed in 1979 the Office of the US Trade Representative (USTR).[1] To square the exigencies of multilateral negotiations with Congressional constitutional prerogatives, in 1974 the 'fast-track' mechanism was developed. Through this procedure, Congress would grant the executive branch negotiating authority and in return the Congress would pre-commit itself to vote in a simple yes–no manner on any proposed agreement as a whole. As Destler has argued, this procedure was useful in that it permitted members of Congress to take positions on the broad contours of trade policy while at the same time absolving them for taking responsibility for the fortunes of particular constituency groups. To the extent that problems arose in specific sectors, for the most part these could be channelled into quasi-judicial procedures such as the ones for antidumping, and Congress could continue to evade responsibility for particular outcomes. In the context of this interbranch balancing act, fast-track authority is now thought to be essential for the successful completion of any multilateral negotiation.

Reductions in trade barriers and transportation and communication costs facilitated the globalisation of the US economy, where the share of international trade (merchandise exports plus imports) in national income doubled from 7 per cent in 1967 to 14 per cent in 1987 and continued to climb to more than 19 per cent in 1997. As the importance of trade increased in the US economy, so did its political salience. The era of Congressional quiescence ended in 1987, when faced with a

---

[1] For an excellent treatment of this history, see Destler (1995).

Republican president thought insufficiently responsive to growing trade deficits, the Democrat-controlled Congress grew restive and began to reassert its constitutional authority. In some ways, the Omnibus Trade and Competitiveness Act of 1988 harked back to those earlier comprehensive tariffs: although it did not contain new statutory protection, it was more than 1000 pages long, containing a laundry list of special legislation for a variety of sectors and a provision, commonly known as 'Super 301', that put the onus on to the Administration to identify and eliminate, through retaliation if need be, egregious foreign barriers to US exports.

In the decade since, trade policy-making in the US has grown enormously in complexity, driven by an expansion of the trade policy agenda beyond the traditional tariff-setting exercise to include economic issues of greater intellectual subtlety, such as the appropriate role for preferential trade agreements, the increasing interlinkage of trade policy with other political issues such as human rights and environmental protection, and the proliferation of new actors including sub-federal governments and non-government organisations (NGOs). Moreover, the President currently lacks fast-track trade authority, greatly circumscribing the Administration's ability to operate proactively on this agenda.

This growing complexity, combined with a reactive, complainant-driven policy-making apparatus and a cultural emphasis on political access, means that trade policy is increasingly subject to political capture by narrow special interest groups. Moreover, the internal organisation of both the Administration and Congress make it difficult for these institutions to deal constructively with this increase in complexity and pluralism. Ironically, from the standpoint of US self-interest, deepened integration through the multilateral system may offer the best hope of pre-committing domestic policymakers to enlightened policies and avoiding self-inflicted damage. In the end however, even this strategy may be inadequate, if free traders fail to defend a strong, well-reasoned commitment to core principles.

2. The Changing Bias of Trade Protection

Despite the rise of the 'new issues', the old issue of protection remains central to the US trade policy agenda. And although many non-Americans might have difficulty believing it, the last decade has actually seen progress on this front, though at a diplomatic price.

Trade policy was an important issue in the 1980 presidential election, for the incumbent president, Jimmy Carter, steadfastly refused to give in to industry pleas for protection. This changed with the election of Ronald Reagan who, in the words of his Treasury secretary James A. Baker III, 'grant[ed] more import relief to US industry than any of his predecessors in more than half a century,' extending special protection to a variety of manufacturing industries, most notably the automobile sector, which cost the US economy billions of dollars.[2]

Political emphasis increasingly shifted from import protection to export promotion in succeeding administrations as Reagan-era protections were removed, and instead action was redirected to the elimination of foreign barriers to US exports. In some cases, this was a logical response to a set of incentives embodied in US law. For example, the Foreign Corrupt Practices Act prohibits US firms from bribery and other corrupt business practices, putting them at a competitive disadvantage to rivals unfettered by similar constraints. Unable to make use of private side-payments to ease entry into restricted markets, US firms turn to the USTR for governmental assistance, making market access a public policy issue. Unfortunately, at times the degree of political capture has been such that market access for particular firms, not market liberalisation *per se*, has become the implicit goal of public policy. For example, US firms have used government pressure to force their way into foreign oligopolies, and having secured a

---

[2] Remarks of Secretary of the Treasury James A. Baker III at the Institute for International Economics, Washington, 14 September 1987.

share of oligopoly rents, then lobbied *against* further pressure to open the market. Hence trade policy has been privatised. One implication of improved international codes on corruption could be a reduction in domestic political pressure on the US government to pursue unilateralist market-opening policies.

Whatever the reasons, this late 1980s redirection of US trade policy away from protection and toward market-opening abroad could arguably be defended as globally welfare-enhancing in that it aimed at ratcheting downward the global incidence of trade barriers, rather than erecting new restraints. (The counter-argument is that bilateral activism reduced the interests of exporters in market opening through global trade negotiations and thereby ultimately retarded, not promoted, liberalisation globally. A similar argument could be made with respect to the subsequent pursuit of preferential trade agreements.) Either way, there was a diplomatic price to be paid: countries such as Japan and Korea, which were subjected to bilateral negotiations about what had been previously considered 'domestic' economic institutions and practices, regarded these as intrusive in a way that they would not have regarded simple application of protection against their exports.

This decade-long movement away from import protection is now in jeopardy, buffeted by two forces. One source of pressure is the rise of the US trade deficit to historically unprecedented levels driven by relatively robust US growth, especially relative to Asia. In spite of a predicted slowdown, the consensus of professional forecasters is that the US will grow more rapidly than Japan and much of the rest of Asia for at least three consecutive years (1997–1999) – a reversal of a decades-old pattern.[3] This means that despite slowing growth, the US trade deficit is likely to expand. The merchandise trade deficit set a historical record in 1998 and may hit an annualised rate of $300 billion in 1999. Growing trade imbalances in the context of slowing growth could affect the political responses to recovery from the crisis in the US, especially if America's unprecedented expansion were to slow and unemployment were to rise. Already

---

[3] See Blue Chip Economic Indicators, February 1999 and Financial Times Currency Forecaster, February 1999.

we see this phenomenon with regard to the steel industry, and in the Clinton Administration's growing calls for 'burden sharing' on the part of the European Union (EU). As one Congressman succinctly put it, 'The US trade deficit is at an all-time high because of our government's irresponsible trade policy.'[4]

Indeed, comprehensive statistical analysis of more than 1,500 USTR actions over a decade and parts or all of four Presidential Administrations found that the level of bilateral trade imbalances is the single best predictor of US trade policy behaviour.[5] The USTR pays more attention to countries with which the US runs large bilateral trade deficits and is more likely to undertake actions that could end in retaliation against those countries. Thus, on the basis of past behaviour, one would expect the growing US trade deficit to be accompanied by increasing trade policy activism. This has already proved true in the case of the steel industry, and more can be expected based on likely patterns of adjustment.[6]

The complication is that the international institutional context has changed and profoundly so. The formation of the World Trade Organisation (WTO) has greatly inhibited the US' ability to use Section 301, or the newly revived 'Super 301', to pry open foreign markets. Before, the US stood as judge, jury and prosecutor, ready to impose retaliation when target countries did not submit, cognisant that denial of access to the lucrative US market could not be successfully challenged in the dysfunctional dispute settlement system of the GATT, the WTO's predecessor. Now, under the WTO's far stronger dispute settlement mechanism, the US is highly constrained in its ability to impose WTO-consistent unilateral trade retaliation. Thus in the primary field of trade policy, the US government finds itself subject to growing demands for action without recourse to its traditional remedies.

---

[4] Office of Representative Sherrod Brown, 'Brown: Increased Trade Deficit Points to Failed U.S. Trade Policies,' 17 July 1998.

[5] See Noland (1997).

[6] See Noland *et al.* (1998).

3. New Issues and Players

For US trade policymakers, the headaches do not stop here. The trade policy agenda has been greatly broadened and action has been greatly complicated by three interrelated phenomena: the rise of new issues, the use of trade policy for new purposes, and the mobilisation of new participants in policy formation.

With respect to the first, a number of issues stand out:
- the appropriate role (if any) for preferential trade agreements
- the linkage between trade and human or labour rights, sometimes described as the 'social clause' issue
- the linkage between trade and the environment
- the relationship between trade and competition policy; and the issue of transborder investment.

Another set of issues relating to the linkage between trade and technological advance, particularly in the form of electronic commerce and biotechnology and genetically altered organisms, is beginning to make an impact. The linkage between trade and social issues, on the one hand, and trade and the environment, on the other, is further complicated by the use of trade restrictions as a mechanism for enforcing compliance with other agreements that are otherwise not trade-related.

Not surprisingly, this broadening of the agenda has been accompanied by an increase in the number of participants in policy-making. In the US, this has primarily taken two forms. One is the application of economic sanctions or boycotts against foreign countries by sub-federal governments or quasi-governmental institutions such as public pension funds. The other is the mobilisation of NGOs, especially environmental NGOs, not traditionally involved in trade policy-making. These groups, together with the more traditional business lobbies and unions, are now known collectively as 'civil society'.

The issue of trade and competition policy is the most technical of the new issues, with respect to both legal and economic principles, and the one with the least political resonance. Within the US there is little intellectual consensus as to what the goals of a desirable international competition policy might be beyond prohibiting horizontal collusive practices such as cartels. Although the topic is of relevance to a wide range of producers, the most active have been the import-competing firms, who regard competition policy as prospectively a much less protection-friendly alternative to the existing, and WTO-consistent, antidumping laws. (There is also some evidence that AD actions have facilitated anticompetitive behaviour – another reason to prefer them to the application of competition policy.) The intellectual debate has been hijacked by lawyers arguing that the goal of trade policy ought to be 'market access,' not 'efficiency'. Indeed, some go so far as to argue that these putative differences in orientation demonstrate that trade and competition policies are fundamentally incompatible.

Within the government, the bureaucracy is split: the Antitrust Division of the Justice Department fears that any multilateral accord would amount to a dumbing down of US law, weakening US antitrust practices, whereas the USTR, stung by its defeat in the WTO in the Kodak–Fuji case, opposes narrowing antidumping laws in the interests of its import-competing clients. The import-competing sectors and their hired guns are fully prepared to mobilise to block any weakening of antidumping law, and unless there is a significant shift in domestic politics, it is hard to envision much constructive activity on this issue emanating from the US in the foreseeable future.

The NAFTA Debate

In contrast to the trade and competition policy debate that takes place within the Washington Beltway, the 'social clause' and environmental protection are hot-button political issues in the US, first coming to the fore during the debate over the North American Free Trade Agreement (NAFTA). Indeed, Destler (1998) argues that NAFTA was a breakpoint that revealed the inadequacies of the 'game' played between Congress and the Administration, which for the previous five decades had been reasonably successful in forestalling product-specific protectionism of the Smoot–Hawley type.

The original impetus for NAFTA in 1990 had come from Mexico, where President Carlos Salinas de Gotari saw it as a mechanism for pre-committing future Mexican governments to liberal economic policies. It was taken up with enthusiasm by US President George Bush who agreed with Salinas' analysis and saw the agreement as a means of addressing a longstanding foreign policy problem as well as a useful bargaining chip with respect to the EU in the context of the Uruguay Round negotiation. The NAFTA proposal, however, generated a firestorm of opposition, especially from a wide range of NGOs. There were many reasons for this. In narrow economic terms, a free trade agreement with a large labour-abundant country would bind the US to something approximating global free trade, and American labour unions consequently felt threatened by it. More broadly, an agreement with Mexico provided NAFTA opponents with an easily graspable target, subject to latent feelings of racism and chauvinism far more tangible than an abstract commitment such as most-favoured-nation treatment in the GATT.

Whatever the basis of the opposition, Bill Clinton, then the centrist Democratic presidential candidate, attempted to square the circle by rejecting the agreement negotiated by the Bush Administration in favour of NAFTA-plus, which would include labour and environmental provisions, and eventually a small regional development bank, in order to obtain the support of key Democratic Party constituent groups.

Even with the labour and environmental side agreements and the development bank, in November 1993 the new Clinton Administration was able to muster votes from only 40 per cent of Democrats in the House of Representatives. The legislation passed on the basis of an overwhelming majority of Republicans supporting the legacy of ex-President Bush. The fact that less than half of the Democrats in the House of Representatives supported NAFTA energised the anti-NAFTA NGOs, who quickly broadened their agenda in opposition to subsequent trade legislation. The American Federation of Labor–Congress of Industrial Organizations (AFL–CIO), the American union umbrella group, mobilised significantly on the workers' rights issue, and is widely credited with successfully lobbying Congress in 1997 to defeat a bill granting the President 'fast-track' negotiating authority without strong provisions requiring the inclusion of workers' rights issues in any trade negotiation. Another attempt to win fast-track similarly failed in 1998. As a consequence of this defeat, the Administration's capability to act proactively in such venues as the Asia-Pacific Economic Cooperation (APEC) forum, the Free Trade Area of the Americas (FTAA) initiative, and new negotiations under the auspices of the WTO, has been constrained.

Labour and Human Rights Clauses

Recognising that there is not a perfect mapping between 'low wage countries' and 'countries with substandard labour practices' or 'poor human rights records,' the US debate over the inclusion of labour or human rights clauses in trade agreements centres on whether such provisions are more likely to encourage improvements in partner countries or simply become a mechanism for implementing protection against imports from developing countries – without achieving the desired improvements in worker or human rights. The question of whether the US would find willing negotiating partners on the other side of the table appears to be almost entirely absent from the domestic debate, as is the issue of whether the imposition of protection would contribute to the improvement of workers' or human rights in the partner country, or indeed might even worsen the situation.

There is weak evidence to support the notion that the inclusion of worker's rights provisions in international trade agreements might not be captured by protectionist interests in the US. Since 1984, a workers' rights provision (along with a provision relating to the protection of intellectual property rights) has been part of the US Generalized System of Preferences (GSP) programme which extends duty-free treatment to some imports from developing countries. The law permits the US government to terminate or suspend the duty-free treatment of imports from countries determined to permit the denial of workers' rights. Elliott (1998) analysed petitions (filed mainly by the AFL–CIO or human rights NGOs) requesting that GSP benefits be suspended owing to denial of workers' rights and found that the pattern of filing did not appear to support the hypothesis that import protection was the intention. Even though only a small volume of imports is eligible for the programme, petitioning activity was intense, including petitions against countries, such as oil producers, that did not receive and could not be plausibly be expected to receive any future benefits under the programme. Moreover, the pattern of acceptance of petitions for review revealed a negative correlation between petition acceptance rates and indicators of political freedom developed by disinterested parties. On the other hand, there was not much evidence that suspension or termination of GSP privileges had contributed to the improvement of workers' rights.

Obviously, experience with the GSP programme does not necessarily indicate how workers' rights provisions in broader trade agreements would work, with respect either to use at home or efficacy abroad. In monetary terms, the GSP stakes are peanuts, for the GSP programme excludes the large and potentially sensitive textile and apparel sector, the competitive need threshold means that countries are dropped from the programme once they can export in significant volume, and communist countries such as China are excluded entirely. If larger volumes of trade, or trade in politically sensitive sectors, or trade with countries such as China were subject to social clause provisions, the pattern of behaviour in the US and abroad could be significantly different.

Trade Policy and Environmental Protection

The linkage between trade policy and environmental protection occurs in several ways. The most obvious, and least controversial, is when goods directly threaten the importing country's environment, for example by acting as a delivery system for non-native pests. In principle, these sorts of cases can be handled through existing or suitably elaborated WTO phytosanitary provisions. A second, and more difficult, case is that of transborder pollution. Here imposition of import restraints is a decided second-best strategy to addressing the negative externality directly. Moreover, these cases could potentially violate the WTO's non-discrimination provisions as well as the conventional interpretation of 'like products' and its prohibition of discrimination on the basis of production techniques. A third and even more contentious problem relates to 'psychological' externalities, as manifested in the US Marine Mammal Protection Act aimed at protecting dolphins or the EU's attempt to ban the importation of furs from animals caught using leg-hold traps.

A final linkage between trade policy and the environment occurs when the imposition of trade restrictions is specified as a mechanism to obtain compliance with multilateral environmental agreements (MEAs) that may have no direct bearing on trade. Examples of such agreements include the International Whaling Convention (IWC) and the Montreal Convention on Chlorofluorocarbons. The Convention on International Trade in Endangered Species (CITES) does concern international trade, but is essentially of the same ilk. Indeed, it is not hard to imagine similar issues arising in the future through MEAs addressing global public goods issues such as atmospheric ozone depletion and broad issues of biodiversity. It is also not hard to imagine a multilateral agreement in the WTO to make congruent the pursuit of competing international goals in the trade and environmental arenas. Indeed, this issue is already under discussion in the WTO's Committee on Trade and Environment. The issues relating to 'psychological' externalities are another matter altogether, however.

By definition, these issues are value-laden, non-rational, and not particularly amenable to negotiation. In the US, the issues have greatly complicated trade policy-making. Interagency policy-making bodies within the government have been expanded to include agencies such as the Environmental Protection Agency and the National Oceanic and Atmospheric Administration, giving them a voice not only in the formation of environment-related trade policies, but in the whole panoply of trade issues, increasing the prospect of cross-issue logrolling. Moreover, the 'psychological' externality issues have proved to be useful tools in mobilising environmental NGOs. The real problem here is that the NGOs have resorted to litigation through the court system to obtain particular policy outcomes. In the tuna–dolphin case, it was NGO litigation on the basis of the Marine Mammal Protection Act that generated the policy outcome eventually leading to the Mexican victory against the

US in the WTO. In the sea turtles case, it was NGO litigation on the basis of the Endangered Species Protection Act which forced the federal government to ban the importation of shrimp not captured using nets that exclude sea turtle, resulting in Malaysia, Pakistan, and Thailand winning a case against the US in the WTO. In a nutshell, these cases demonstrate the new complexity – a novel concern and three new classes of actors in the formation of trade policy: non-economic agencies within the government, NGOs, and the courts.

Economic Sanctions and Foreign Policy Goals

Similar issues are raised by the use of economic sanctions to achieve foreign policy goals. Like one aspect of the trade–environment linkage, one can imagine sanctions in the context of multilateral agreements on global public goods, such as in the case of UN-sanctioned trade embargoes. The problem in the US, however, is not these multilaterally imposed embargoes, but what President Clinton described as increasingly 'sanctions-happy' federal and sub-federal governments.[7] Not only are direct embargoes at issue, but sanctions against third parties that decline to participate in boycotts, as in the Helms–Burton Law which penalises firms doing business in Cuba, and the State of Massachusetts' sanctions against companies doing business in Burma which is being investigated by a WTO panel convened at the request of Japan and the EU. It is not much of a stretch to say that, in the post-Cold War era, sanctions have become the first-resort 'feel-good' policy of moral preening. The US currently imposes economic sanctions against 26 countries accounting for more than half of the world's population.[8] The problem is that these sanctions are seldom effective and can impose terrible costs on populations that have little, if any, control over the actions of their governments. Moreover, the economic costs to the US are hidden: a partial equilibrium analysis by Hufbauer *et al.* (1997) concludes that sanctions reduce US exports by $20 billion or 200,000 high-paying jobs annually. Even more disturbing is the

---

[7] Gary Clyde Hufbauer, 'Sanctions-Happy USA,' *International Economic Policy Brief* 98-4, Washington: Institute for International Economics.

[8] For an encyclopaedic analysis of economic sanctions, see Hufbauer *et al.* (1999).

willingness of state and municipal governments to join in the politics of moral outrage, and the unwillingness of the Clinton Administration to take them on politically or challenge them constitutionally through the courts on the basis of the federal government's exclusive right to regulate foreign trade.

The Case of the MAI

Perhaps the most striking example of the newly mobilised political forces in trade policy-making was the collapse in 1998 of the Multilateral Investment Initiative (MAI).[9] Stymied by the opposition of developing countries in the WTO, the developed countries began in 1995 to negotiate a multilateral investment liberalisation accord in the Organisation for Economic Co-operation and Development (OECD). The core principles of the initiative – national treatment and most-favoured-nation – were borrowed from the international trade régime, but negotiators were far from agreement on a wide range of issues and the draft text was full of bracketed language, footnotes expressing national delegations' concerns, and national exceptions. In February 1997, this text was leaked to Public Citizen, a Washington-based NGO that had earlier made its mark with its hysterical opposition to the NAFTA, the Uruguay Round, the fast-track proposal, the African Growth and Opportunity Act, and every other recent attempt to liberalise the US trade regime. A kind of intellectual Gresham's Law took hold on the internet with a transnational coalition of NGOs making outlandish and apocalyptic claims about what was admittedly a work in progress. In the US, a diverse set of groups, including the AFL–CIO, the Sierra Club, the Western Governors Association, and the Women's Division of the United Methodist Church were among the organisations that came out against the treaty – which was still being negotiated.

The US government, along with its OECD counterparts, was clearly caught flat-footed and was slow to respond. And, in April 1998, the OECD announced that the negotiations would be suspended for six months. For all intents and purposes the MAI is dead, though one can debate whether it was due to self-

---

[9] See Kobrin (1998) for a fascinating account of the collapse of the MAI negotiations.

inflicted wounds or represents the first major casualty inflicted by a global coalition of NGOs. The mobilisation of NGOs in the US has clearly reached the point to which it can have decisive effects on policy outcomes.

4. Constraints on Unilateralism

Given US tendencies toward trade policy unilateralism in both old and new guises, it is hard to understate just how profoundly the formation of the WTO has constrained US policy. Despite the Clinton Administration's recent resuscitation of 'Super 301' this instrument, along with other similar tools, has to all intents and purposes been rendered ineffective by the formation of the WTO and its improved dispute settlement mechanism. In the past, unilateral action to close the lucrative US market was a credible threat that the USTR could deploy in its bilateral negotiations with trade partners over these partners' alleged barriers. Now the threat is almost entirely non-credible. During recent disputes, USTR officials scrambled to identify products or services in which access to the US market was not bound by WTO commitments, and were hard pressed to come up with much. The one recent case, which did play out according to the old threat and counterthreat script, was a shipping dispute between the US and Japan in which the issue (harbour fees and procedures) was not covered under the WTO and the principal bureaucratic protagonists were not the WTO-socialised USTR and its counterpart, the Japanese Ministry of Trade and Industry, but rather the two countries' respective shipping regulators.

Despite this impact on trade policy, the WTO appears to have little political salience in the US beyond the traditional sovereignty-obsessed nationalism of the far right, and the more recent, though equally paranoid, concerns of the NGO left, both tapping deep cultural veins of sensitivity regarding popular access to political decision-making and suspicion toward concentration of political power. However, for most Americans, the WTO is best known for its work on astonishingly minor issues such as bananas. This is probably just as well, because in the US–EU dispute over bananas, the traditional special interest politics of trade policy has inadvertently stumbled into principle.

Bananas and WTO Rules

With the exception of a few trees in South Florida or Hawaii, the US does not produce bananas. It is, however, home to Chiquita Brands, a large banana-producing firm known in Washington as much for its large political contributions as for its catchy advertising jingle. Chiquita produces bananas in Latin America and has long complained that it is disadvantaged by the EU import quota allocation scheme which grants preferences to former colonies of France and the UK in Africa, the Caribbean, and the Pacific where distribution is dominated by EU-based firms.

The US government has repeatedly gone to bat for Chiquita, together with allies from the affected Latin American countries, winning cases against the EU in 1993, 1994, and most recently in 1997 on the basis of the EU's preference scheme under Article XIII of the WTO agreement. In response to its last defeat under the new and strengthened dispute settlement system, the EU refused to consult with the US or the Latin American complainants and instead made minor alterations to its banana importation regime, allegedly bringing its practices into compliance with its WTO obligations. This is when money politics was elevated into high principle. The US cried foul and via WTO Article XXII began the legal procedure required under US domestic law (Section 301) to apply retaliation, which EU trade commissioner Sir Leon Brittan described as US 'unilateralism at its worst'. The EU claimed that there was a 'disagreement' as to whether its actions had brought it into conformity with its WTO obligations and then requested the US to go through another round of WTO dispute settlement (under Article XXI.5), postponing retaliation, undertaking surveillance, and inviting, as USTR Charlene Barshevsky characterised it, 'an endless loop of litigation.'

The crux of the dispute is a lacuna in the WTO rules as to how a country brings its practices into conformity and who determines if this has been achieved. The obvious difficulty is that if losers are able to define 'disagreement,' then dispute settlement is hamstrung, and the world is more or less back to the dysfunction and dispute settlement system of the GATT. An obvious solution would be to have the original panel, or an arbitrator selected from the original panel, review the dispute and rule whether the contention rose to the level of a legitimate disagreement to be handled under Section XXI.5, or whether the loser's claim was frivolous and retaliation could proceed under Section XXII.

What can be the objection to so obvious a solution? First, it would require a formal amendment of WTO rules which could prove contentious, and in any event could not be done quickly. The real issue is that the banana case has pointed out a potentially devastating flaw in the WTO dispute settlement rules. Although the thought of the banana case evokes slapstick humour and bad puns, far more is at stake both economically and politically in the US–EU beef hormone fracas and the US–Canadian magazine dispute. In both cases, WTO panels have issued ambiguously worded reports that would appear to be ripe for the same kind of conflict as has occurred in the banana case. Moreover, third parties, fearing US unilateralism and attacks on their own trade practices, have allied with the EU's stalling tactics, clearly seeing the banana case as prospectively precedent-setting.

In the end, the banana dispute may be a blessing in disguise, permitting issues of principle to be settled in the context of a low-stakes dispute rather than in the context of the immediate alternatives of beef hormones and magazines which could arouse far deeper public passions. But whatever the outcome of this case, the WTO Trade Ministerial in Seattle in November is likely to be a focus of a high-visibility attempt by the AFL–CIO and NGOs to influence the world trade agenda. Already some are talking of the US exercising its right of withdrawal under Article XV which could be triggered by the five-year review mandated in the US' implementing legislation.

5. Fast-track Authority and the Role of the Judiciary

The US government faces an increasingly complex set of issues combining traditional trade problems with a growing set of economic, environmental, and diplomatic concerns. At the same time that the substance of policy-making is growing in complexity, the process of policy formation has witnessed the mobilisation of new groups and interests. All three branches of government appear to be reacting to these developments in a rather *ad hoc* manner.

For most of this century, the locus of trade policy-making has rested in the executive branch of the government. At the policy level, responsibility lies primarily with the USTR, historically a small and relatively weak organisation in bureaucratic terms, within the Executive Office of the President. The traditional criticism of the bureaucratic organisation of US trade policy is that it is fragmented: although USTR bears the primary responsibility for negotiating trade agreements, it bears no real responsibility for their implementation or the adjustment costs that arise from them. These functions are delegated to other organs of the executive branch.

In keeping with its brief as a trade policy *negotiating* unit, the organisation is staffed largely by lawyers who are far more comfortable with the French-derived jargon of diplomacy than the algebraic formulations of economic welfare theorems. Within USTR, the office of the Chief Economist consists of a single individual assisted by two colleagues seconded from other organisations. This staffing pattern has two real effects. First, the organisation does not have the resources to make economic assessments of industry-submitted complaints and claims nor evaluate the economic implications of alternative policies. The inability to do economic analysis means that priorities are set according to non-economic considerations, which increases the likelihood of political capture by special interests. Second, a culture of litigation has developed in which legally-enforceable trade agreements, not improvements in economic efficiency, are the prime objective. Together, these bureaucratic characteristics encourage activity, though not necessarily economically rational activity.

Perhaps this did not make much difference during the Cold War, when the imperative of East–West confrontation subsumed all other foreign policy questions. But in the post-Cold War era, the emphasis on tactics over strategy has been crippling. The impression is that there is no real sense of priorities among competing claims on resources.

Perhaps it is too much to expect such priority setting. One could accept the notion that USTR is essentially just the negotiating arm of the executive branch, responsible only for attaining the goals set by others and itself not responsible for developing any overarching strategy for trade policy. If that is the case, then the blame lies squarely in the White House. It is interesting to note that the last two significant accomplishments in US trade policy, the creation of NAFTA and the WTO, had their origins either during the Cold War (WTO) or in its immediate aftermath (NAFTA).

Fast-track trade authority is regarded as *sine qua non* for the conclusion of any future multilateral agreement. Probably the most troubling aspect of the Clinton Administration's trade policy decision-making has been its inability to secure fast-track authority from the Congress. This has its origins in the Administration's decision in 1994 to remove fast-track authorisation from the legislation implementing the Uruguay Round agreement, out of fear that its inclusion could jeopardise the broader legislation's' passage.[10] The political calculus revolves largely around the issues of the 'social clause' and environmental protection; a certain segment of Democratic lawmakers might be persuaded to support fast-track authorisation if their concerns were met; another group of Republican Congressmen could be expected to defect from supporting the legislation if strong language on these issues was included. One

---

10
    See Destler (1997) for a highly readable account of what, in other hands, would be a mind-numbing description of the political manoeuvring over fast-track.

could imagine a variety of fast-track bills being passed depending on the outcome of the 2000 election – a 'Democrat' version which would require the Administration to include labour and environment provisions in any trade legislation or a 'Republican' version which, in an extreme form, might prohibit the Administration from addressing these issues.

If leadership on trade issues does not emanate from the executive branch, what about the Congress? The prospects do not look promising. First, as Destler (1998) argues, the committee structure of Congress (specifically, the control of trade legislation by the fiscally-oriented House Ways and Means Committee and the Senate Finance Committee) does not lend itself to the consideration of cross-cutting issues such as trade and the environment. Second, at least in the 1997 fast-track debate in which assessments of the experience with NAFTA played a critical role, key individual members of the House and Senate with considerable expertise and interest in the core issues had retired, and as a consequence, the debate was characterised by 'passionate advocacy of ancillary issues' such as labour standards, the environment, and human rights.

Finally, recent empirical research into Congressional voting patterns on trade issues confirms what was known all along, namely that 'trade policy is for sale by the House of Representatives.'[11] Members' receipts of political contributions by union and business political action committees (PACs) are strongly associated with votes on major trade legislation, with union contributions appearing to be particularly effective (possibly because of a greater ability to deliver votes as well as money at election time). The importance of contributions is such that without business PACs, NAFTA would not have passed in the House of Representatives. Trade policy has indeed been privatised.

This leaves the judiciary. Historically, the judiciary has been the least important of the three branches of government in the formation of trade policy. Recent forays into trade policy-making have amounted to decisions forcing the government to enforce domestic laws (the Marine Mammal Protection Act, the

---

11
    See Baldwin and Magee (1998).

Endangered Species Protection Act) that conflict with international obligations under the WTO.

Moreover, there is little reason to believe that the judiciary could be expected to play a constructive role in the future as it has shown little comprehension of political reality in the recent past. In a decision that was truly remarkable in its naiveté, the Supreme Court ruled that subjecting a sitting President to a civil suit would not unduly distract from the business of governance. This ruling allowed Paula Jones' lawsuit alleging sexual harassment to go forward, which eventually led to the first impeachment of an elected President in US history and resulted in a massive distraction from the proper task of government.

Recent decisions against tobacco and gun-makers may well signal an era of renewed judicial activism in the US, as litigants attempt to use the courts to impose fiat solutions to complex and controversial social problems. The last time the courts did this, mandating the legalisation of abortion in 1973, they set in motion a political dispute which has given rise to the closest thing the US has experienced to a sustained domestic terrorism campaign in a quarter century. The thought of the judiciary 'solving' the trade and environment or trade and labour or trade and human rights problems is not pleasing to contemplate.

6. Conclusion

For 50 years beginning in 1934, the US Congress, in effect, evaded its Constitutional duty by allowing the President to take the lead in formulating trade policy. This system of acquiescence with oversight more or less successfully addressed the tendency of the Congress to engage in protectionist log-rolling exercises when setting tariffs by absolving the Congress of the primary responsibility for trade outcomes for particular industries, either by subsuming tariffs into large packages or channelling demands for protection into quasi-judicial remedies such as the antidumping procedure.

This system began to fray in the mid-1980s under the strain of record trade deficits and partisan political rivalries of a divided government. The system's demise received a further impetus in the early 1990s with the fight over NAFTA and the dramatic increase in demands on trade policy both in the form of new issues (preferential trade agreements, the social clause, the environment, competition policy) and new participants, especially anti-trade NGOs.

The result has been a trade policy marked by little overall strategic coherence and, as a consequence, little public appeal. The debate over trade policy has been reduced almost to pure tactics, and the pro-liberalisation forces within the Congress and Administration have been badly outplayed. The AFL–CIO and the NGOs are likely to make another push at the time of the WTO trade ministerial in Seattle.

One can imagine the US pursuing coherent trade policies. One alternative would be a policy that explicitly recognises the centrality of the new issues to the agenda and responds both substantively and organisationally to deal with the new reality. Another equally coherent approach would marginalise the influence of the new players, insulating traditional market access issues from the new demands. Both responses require a degree of intellectual honesty that the political class appears unable to muster and, in the absence of leadership, the US polity is badly split. It is unlikely that either strategy is sustainable, without a significant shift in public sentiment. This would appear to be a recipe for continued drift and continued use of trade policy by narrow special interests for particular ends. In such an environment, international agreements, which could constrain the abuse of domestic policy formation, could be a useful way to pre-commit authorities to relatively enlightened policies. Even this approach may prove unsustainable, however, if supporters of a liberal international system do not demonstrate the courage of their convictions.

References

Baldwin, R.E., and C.S. Magee (1998) 'Is Trade Policy for Sale?', NBER Working Paper No. W6376, Cambridge, MA: National Bureau of Economic Research.

Destler, I.M. (1995): *American Trade Politics*, 3rd edn, Washington: Institute for International Economics.

Destler, I.M. (1997: 'Renewing Fast-Track Legislation,' *Policy Analyses in International Economics*, 50, Washington: Institute for International Economics.

Destler, I.M. (1998): 'Congress and Foreign Trade,' in Robert A. Pastor and Rafael Fernandez de Castro (eds.), *The Controversial Pivot: The US Congress and North America*, Brookings Institution Press, pp. 121-46.

Elliott, K.A. (1998): 'Preferences for Workers? Worker Rights and the US Generalised System of Preferences,' Paper presented at the conference on Globalization and Inequality, Calvin College, Grand Rapids, MI, 28–30 May.

Hufbauer, G.C., K.A. Elliott, T. Cyrus and E. Winston (1997): 'US Economic Sanctions: Their Impact on Trade, Jobs, and Wages,' Washington: Institute for International Economics.

Hufbauer, G.C., J.J. Schott and K.A. Elliott (1999): *Economic Sanctions Reconsidered*, 3rd edn, Washington: Institute for International Economics.

Kobrin, S.J. (1998): 'The MAI and the Clash of Globalisations,' *Foreign Affairs*, 112, 97–109.

Noland, M. (1997): 'Chasing Phantoms,' *International Organisation*, 51:3, 365–87.

Noland, M, LiGang Liu, S. Robinson, and Zhi Wang (1998) 'Global Economic Effects of the Asian Currency Devaluation,' *Policy Analyses in International Economics*, 56, Washington: Institute for International Economics.

Ethics and the Arms Trade

Philip Towle

The disarmament which followed the collapse of the Soviet Union was as rapid as that which occurred after the two world wars. As a consequence the British defence industry, which continues to occupy a stronger position in the international market place than most other UK industries, now faces a distinctly uncertain future.

With the contraction of Britain's military forces, arms exports have become even more essential to the industry and, indirectly, to British defence preparedness and influence, while at the same time becoming the increasing focus of political controversy and public debate.

In large part the controversy reflects the attempt to achieve an 'ethical' approach to arms sales. This, however, has potential to inhibit the development of the nation's technological base, and thus undermine defence and foreign policy objectives. The rationale for such an approach therefore requires rigorous examination.

The industry's critics claim that arms sales assist repressive states in perpetrating human rights abuses, that they cause wars, that they result in increased war casualties and that they impede economic development. But these claims are either false or need qualification.

Repressive states do not need expensive high-tech modern weaponry to abuse their citizens or to wage genocide; such weaponry is unsuitable for that purpose. Arms sales can be destabilising but they can also be stabilising; the ultimate underlying causes are always political. Moreover, there is no evidence of a correlation between the levels of arms exports and the numbers of casualties. Finally, while weapons purchases may direct resources away from civilian uses in the Third World, they quite clearly have not prevented economic development.

There may be a case for banning the export of small arms, which can be used for purposes of repression and easily fall into the hands of criminal organisations. But those weapons can be used to deter aggression and to repair imbalances of power, as well as to initiate conflict and to undermine stability. The effect of arms sales depends upon the quality of the political judgement of the exporting state.

In complex real-life situations ethical judgements require fine distinctions and complicated calculations; ironically those in Whitehall and Westminster who wrestle with complexities of alternative courses of action often come closer to meeting the criteria for genuine moral judgement than those seeking comprehensive bans on arms sales.

The Institute of Economic Affairs
2 Lord North Street, Westminster, London SW1P 3LB
Telephone: 0171 799 3745 Facsimile: 0171 799 2137
E-mail: iea@iea.org.uk Internet: http://www.iea.org.uk

£4.00

ISBN 0-255 36464-2

Living Down the Past:
How Europe can Help Africa Grow
Paul Collier

Western business regards Africa as the world's riskiest region in which to invest. The continent is thus largely excluded from the present rapid process of economic integration. Moreover, during the 1980s much of Africa excluded itself from the global market place through protectionism and statist economic policies. Economic growth has therefore been slow, or negative; this has served to aggravate the risk of civil war which, in turn, has provided a further disincentive to Western investment.

Relations between Western governments and those of sub-Saharan African are now set in a pattern which reinforces the negative attitudes of Western companies towards the continent. The West offers aid in return for economic reform, but even when the proposed measures are introduced, they are often abandoned once the aid has been received.

For reasons of history and self-interest the European Union is best placed to act as an 'agency of restraint': the problems of illegal immigration and drug trafficking which would arise from an explosion of conflict anarchy across sub-Saharan Africa are too serious to ignore, while the continent provides a huge potential market.

The most effective means of assisting those states seriously bent on reform would be a revision to the Lome agreement enabling economic relations between Europe and Africa to be shifted from unilateral concessions to reciprocity. As a consequence, African states would have a series of options - ranging from Lome in its present form to full reciprocal free trade with EU members. States which chose the more ambitious option could expect to become the African pace-setters.

As Botswana - one of the world's fastest growing economies - has demonstrated, economic freedom and market reforms work in Africa, as elsewhere. Over recent decades Africa's record has not been significantly worse than that of Eastern and Central Europe. What has been lacking has been a way of signalling a decisive break with the past. Europe has a role in enabling Africa to signal that break.

The Institute of Economic Affairs
2 Lord North Street, Westminster, London SW1P 3LB
Telephone: 0171 799 3745 Facsimile: 0171 799 2137
E-mail: iea@iea.org.uk Internet: http://www.iea.org.uk   ISBN 0-255 36466-0

£5.00